I0181781

THE ESSENTIAL BOOK OF

Love

SPELLS AND

Magic

Beatrice Aurelia Crowley

Erebus Society

Erebus Society

All rights reserved; no part of this publication may be reproduced or transmitted by any means, electronic, mechanical, photocopying or otherwise, without the prior written permission of the publisher except for the use of brief quotations in a book review.

First published in Great Britain in 2025
Erebus Society

First Edition

Copyright © Beatrice Aurelia Crowley 2025
Book Design Copyright © Erebus Society 2025
Cover Copyright © Ars Corvinus 2025

ISBN: 978-1-912461-76-9

www.ErebusSociety.com

Table of Contens

What is Love Magic?

THE SACRED ART OF LOVE MAGIC

Love is an immensely potent force in the universe, binding souls, intertwining destiny, and shaping the essence of life. Love magic, an esteemed and somewhat contentious aspect of witchcraft, harnesses this deep energy to attract, amplify, heal, and fortify love in its various manifestations—be it romantic, platonic, self-love, or spiritual connection.

Love magic, encompassing murmured prayers over flowers and honey, as well as the binding of hearts with crimson thread and holy vows, has historically been integral to witchcraft, folklore, and spiritual traditions. It is a phenomenon of the heart, imbued with longing, commitment, fervour, and profound emotional metamorphosis.

What, in essence, is love magic? What is its function, and what significance does it hold in relationships, personal empowerment, and emotional healing? Let us examine this captivating and very intimate style of magic, revealing its origins, techniques, and importance within the broader context of the arcane.

UNDERSTANDING LOVE MAGIC

Love magic transcends mere spells for attracting a partner; it is a profound and transforming practice that engages the heart, soul, and energy of interpersonal connections. It may be utilised for:

❀ Attract love - Summoning a soulmate or prospective romantic companion.

❀ Augment passion - Fortifying closeness and desire within an existing relationship.

❀ Heal heartbreak - Alleviating past traumas and reinstating emotional equilibrium.

❀ Enhance self-love — Bolstering confidence and self-esteem.

❀ Establish spiritual ties - Enhancing relationships beyond the corporeal domain.

Love magic operates through intention, emotion, and energetic alignment, facilitating the unobstructed and harmonious flow of love in one's life.

METHODS OF LOVE MAGIC

Candle Love Spells - The application of colour magic amplifies love spells:

❀ Red candles - Passion and yearning

❀ Pink candles symbolise self-love and romantic harmony.

❀ White candles symbolise purity and a connection with one's partner.

Botanical & Floral Sorcery - Roses, jasmine, hibiscus, and lavender are frequently utilised in love potions, charm bags, and baths.

Crystal Love Magic - Gemstones like rose quartz, garnet, and moonstone are utilised to enhance love, attraction, and emotional healing.

Love Potions and Teas - Herbal infusions with cinnamon, vanilla, and damiana to stimulate desire and enhance emotional connections.

Mirror Magic — Contemplating a charged mirror to emanate beauty, confidence, and love-attracting energy.

Love Knots and Thread Magic - Enchantments designed to enhance relationships or summon a soulmate.

Lunar and Aquatic Enchantment - Infusing water with energy under a full moon to sanctify and amplify love vibrations.

ORIGINS AND HISTORY OF LOVE MAGIC

The practice of love magic is as old as humanity. Throughout civilisations, religions, and mystical traditions, love spells, charms, and potions have been employed to ignite romance, sustain commitment, and mend the scars of lost love.

ANCIENT CIVILISATIONS AND LOVE SPELLS

In Ancient Egypt, love magic was extensively performed, frequently invoking Hathor, the goddess of love and joy. Egyptian love spells commonly employed oils, fragrances, and amulets, whilst love charms were etched on papyrus and worn on the person.

In Mesopotamia, the Sumerians and Babylonians invoked Ishtar (Inanna), the goddess of love and fertility, through ritual dances, holy sacrifices, and love potions to enhance and fortify romantic connections.

In Ancient Greece and Rome, love magic was simultaneously feared and admired. Aphrodite (Venus) was venerated in love rituals, with several spells incorporating herbs, honey, and charmed mirrors. The Greeks feared eros magic, fearing that love spells could subvert free will.

CELTIC, NORSE, AND INDIGENOUS TRADITIONS

Celtic Love Magic   The Celts perceived love as intricately connected to nature, employing knot magic, herbal talismans, and lunar ceremonies to fortify relationships. It was believed that sacred wells conferred blessings onto persons in pursuit of genuine love.

Norse Traditions — The Norse employed runic inscriptions and mead-infused potions in their amorous rituals, frequently invoking Freyja, the goddess of love and desire. Love ties were prevalent but necessitated deliberate intention to prevent unforeseen repercussions.

Indigenous Love Magic - Numerous indigenous societies have the belief in soulmates and spiritual love connections, employing songs, carvings, and offerings to summon a destined spouse. Certain traditions employ feathers, stones, and sacred herbs to evoke love.

MEDIEVAL AND RENAISSANCE LOVE MAGIC

Folk Love Magic - In mediaeval Europe, love magic encompassed a blend of Christian, Pagan, and folk traditions. Astute women and shrewd practitioners devised love potions, poppets, and charm bags to attract affection or heal fractured hearts.

Alchemical Love Magic - Renaissance alchemists pursued the "Elixir of Love," amalgamating herbs, metals, and celestial forces to produce potions that intensified attraction and emotional bonds.

Magical Correspondences

These herbs and crystals may be utilised in love spells, potions, charm bags, rituals, and energy work to augment romantic, self-love, and soulmate relationships.

HERBS

APPLE BLOSSOM

Symbolises romance, attraction, and the sweetness of new love. Used in love charms and offerings.

BASIL

Enhances passion and commitment in relationships, often used in love spells and fidelity charms.

CATNIP

Draws affection and playful energy into relationships, used in sachets and attraction spells.

CHAMOMILE

Promotes emotional harmony and peace in relationships, commonly used in love baths and teas.

CINNAMON

Intensifies passion and sexual attraction, often added to love potions and candle spells.

DAMIANA

A powerful aphrodisiac herb that enhances sensuality and strengthens intimate connections.

ELDERFLOWER

Attracts long-lasting love and blessings in relationships, often used in wedding magic.

GARDENIA

Promotes spiritual love, trust, and emotional connection, often infused in oils or perfumes.

GINGER

Adds fiery passion to love spells and encourages boldness in romance.

HIBISCUS

Associated with beauty, attraction, and heightened romantic energy, used in teas and baths.

HONEYSUCKLE

Draws sweet, lasting love and strengthens devotion between partners.

JASMINE

Enhances sensuality, dream connection, and soulmate attraction.

LAVENDER

Encourages love, loyalty, and peaceful relationships, often used in charm bags and spells.

LEMON BALM

Helps in healing heartache and welcoming new love. Used in teas and emotional balancing spells.

MARJORAM

Strengthens love and prevents emotional strain in long-term relationships.

MINT

Brings fresh energy to love and romance, often used in attraction and renewal spells.

ORCHID

A symbol of luxury and deep passion, used in beauty and love enchantments.

ROSE

The ultimate flower of love, representing passion, romance, and emotional healing. Used in nearly all love magic.

ROSEMARY

Strengthens love and commitment, often used in handfasting rituals and fidelity charms.

VANILLA

Adds warmth, attraction, and sensual pleasure to love magic, often used in oils and incense.

CRYSTALS AND MINERALS

AMAZONITE

Encourages open communication and harmony in relationships.

AMETHYST

Promotes emotional balance and spiritual love, strengthening bonds of the soul.

APATITE

(Pink or Blue)

Enhances understanding and deepens emotional connections.

AQUAMARINE

Calms turbulent relationships and strengthens long-term love.

CARNELIAN

Sparks passion, desire, and confidence in romantic pursuits.

CHRYSOPRASE

Promotes forgiveness, heart healing, and the renewal of love.

CLEAR QUARTZ

Amplifies love energy and can be programmed for any love-related intention.

EMERALD

A stone of true love and devotion, deepening bonds and commitment.

FLUORITE
(Pink or Green)

Enhances emotional clarity and removes confusion in love matters.

GARNET

A powerful stone for passion, desire, and rekindling romance.

JADE
(Green or Pink)

Attracts good luck in love and nurtures gentle, long-lasting affection.

KUNZITE

Fosters deep emotional connections and opens the heart to divine love.

LAPIS LAZULI

Encourages honest communication and strengthens soulmate connections.

MALACHITE

Removes emotional blockages and helps release past relationship trauma.

MOONSTONE

A stone of romance and feminine energy, enhancing intuition in love.

MORGANITE

Brings unconditional love, emotional healing, and soulmate attraction.

OPAL

Magnifies desire and seduction, often used in attraction spells.

RHODONITE

Helps heal emotional wounds and encourages self-love and compassion.

ROSE QUARTZ

The ultimate love stone, enhancing romance, self-love, and harmony in relationships.

RUBY

A stone of deep passion, fiery love, and physical attraction.

Calling Upon Divine Powers

GODDESSES TO INVOKE:

Aphrodite: Greek Goddess of passionate, sexual love. Aphrodite's energy can pull loving vibrations toward you, making her ideal for spells of attraction and romance.

Aradia: Italian Queen of the Witches, daughter of Diana. Aradia is a powerful protectress of Witches and can offer strong protection and guidance in your magical workings.

Artemis: Greek Goddess of the Moon and the Hunt. Artemis is a guardian of nature and women, offering protection and strength, especially in matters of independence and self-discovery.

Astarte: Greek Fertility Goddess. Whether you wish to bear children or cultivate a magnificent garden, Astarte can assist in your desires for growth and abundance.

Demeter: Greek Earth Mother archetype. An excellent Goddess to call upon for matters involving birthing and the care of small children, Demeter nurtures and sustains life.

Diana: Roman Moon Goddess and Goddess of the Hunt. Diana is multifaceted, serving as both seductress and mother figure to Witches. She enchants and protects.

Isis: Egyptian Goddess embodying the complete Goddess or Triple Goddess archetype. Isis represents magic, healing, and the mysteries of life and death.

Persephone: Greek Goddess of the Underworld and Harvest. As the daughter of Demeter, Persephone bridges the worlds of life and death, guiding transitions and seasonal cycles.

Selene: Greek Goddess of the Moon and Solutions. Selene brings logical answers and clarity to any problem, illuminating the path forward.

Venus: Roman Goddess of Love and Romance. Venus is the embodiment of beauty and desire, perfect for invoking passionate and romantic love.

GODS TO INVOKE:

Adonis: Greek consort of Aphrodite, also known as "lord." In Phoenician mythology, he is associated with Astarte. Adonis symbolizes rebirth and the cycles of nature. The Roman counterpart is Venus.

Apollo: Greek and Roman God of the Sun, Light, and the Arts. Twin brother of Artemis, Apollo inspires creativity, healing, and prophecy.

Cernunnos: Celtic Horned God and consort of the Lady. Also known as Kernunnos, he is the God of Nature, fertility, and the forest.

Eros: Greek God of Romance and Passionate Love. Eros ignites the fires of desire and deep emotional connections.

Hymen: Greek God of Marriage and commitment. Hymen oversees the sanctity of marriage and long-term relationships, ensuring fidelity and union. His counterpart is Dionysus.

Luce: Italian God of the Sun and Light, soulmate and brother of Diana, father of Aradia. Luce brings illumination, warmth, and clarity.

Osiris: Egyptian God and counterpart of Isis. Osiris represents vegetation, the afterlife, and resurrection, embodying the cycle of life and death.

Pan: Greek God of Nature, the Woods, Laughter, and Passion. Pan embodies the wild, untamed aspects of nature and human desire, bringing joy and ecstasy.

Spells

A Penny for Love

REQUIREMENTS:

❁ One copper penny (preferably an older one)
❁ A well or body of water

INSTRUCTIONS:

Hold the copper penny in your projective hand (the hand you write with).

Visualize you and your partner sharing joyful moments, focusing deeply on the love and happiness between you.

Pour all your positive energy and loving intentions into the penny, feeling the warmth of your love infusing the metal.

Stand near a well or a body of water.

Toss the penny over your right shoulder into the water, while chanting:

"Coin of Venus, copper and bright,
Bind our hearts with love's true light.
Smooth the path we walk each day,
In love's embrace, we'll always stay.
Strengthen our bond, pure and strong,
In harmony, where we belong.
By the powers of water and love,
Bless our union from above.
As this penny sinks below,
Our love will flourish, this we know.
This is our will, as we decree,
Bound in love, so mote it be."

After tossing the penny, close your eyes and visualize the love between you and your partner growing stronger and more harmonious.

Apple Love Spell

REQUIREMENTS:

- ❊ One apple
- ❊ A sewing needle
- ❊ Red thread
- ❊ Pink ribbon

INSTRUCTIONS:

Begin by cutting the apple in half.

Carve your initials on the inside of one half, and the initials of your desired person on the inside of the other half.

Use the sewing needle to loosely thread the red thread through both halves, rejoining them.

Find the tree from which the apple came, or another tree if that's not possible.

Hang the rejoined apple from the tree using the pink ribbon.

Stand before the tree, focusing on your desire.

Chant with intention:

> "Apple of love, from leaf to tree,
> Bind our hearts, and let it be.
> Draw him close, entwine our fate,
> Love's sweet magic, now create."

Visualize your love growing and flourishing just as the apple once did on the tree.

Leave the apple hanging as a symbol of your binding spell.

Attract a Date

REQUIREMENTS:

❀ Dates
❀ Powdered sugar
❀ Maple syrup or honey (in a squirt bottle)
❀ Tin foil

INSTRUCTIONS:

Light a pink or red candle to symbolize love and attraction.

Arrange love-related items such as rose quartz, heart charms, or flowers around your space.

Place a date on the table and carve your initials into it.

Sprinkle a circle of powdered sugar around the date to symbolize sweetness and removing obstacles.

With your finger, write the reasons for your dating troubles in the powdered sugar circle. Blow the powder away, visualizing the removal of these obstacles.

On the tin foil, use the syrup or honey to write three positive qualities you seek in a partner.

Roll the date in the sticky syrup or honey, erasing the words as the date absorbs the sweetness.

Hold the date in your hands and focus on your intention.

Chant:

"Sweetness drawn from nature's core,
Attract to me love I adore.
Erase the troubles, draw them near,
A perfect match, sincere and dear."

Place the date in your mouth and let it roll across your tongue.

Visualize your ideal partner coming to you, feeling the energy of attraction building.

Blow out the candle, sealing the energy of the spell.

Dispose of the tin foil and any leftover ingredients, giving thanks to the energies that have aided you.

Attract the Love of Your Life

REQUIREMENTS:

❋ A sampler size of your favorite scent
❋ A pink candle
❋ A tack or toothpick

INSTRUCTIONS:

Carve a heart into the pink candle using a tack or toothpick.

Light the candle in a window where it will receive moonlight, preferably during a full moon.

Place the scent container in front of the candle.

As the candle burns, chant:

"Venus, grant me the love that I lack,
Through this scent, my mate attract!"

Allow the candle to burn out naturally, infusing the scent with the power of your intention.

Carry the scent with you, applying a little whenever you go out or expect to meet new people.

To enhance the magic, repeat the invocation as you apply the scent:

"Venus, grant me love so true,
Through this scent, my mate pursue."

Chant to Seal the Spell:

"By moon's light and Venus' grace,
Love shall find me, heart to embrace.
With this scent, my charm renew,
Attract my love, so pure and true."

Banish Lovers' Jealousy

REQUIREMENTS:

❀ Ylang-ylang essential oil
❀ Myrrh essential oil
❀ Coriander essential oil
❀ Oil burner

INSTRUCTIONS:

Perform this spell in the bedroom.

Open the window to allow the negative energy to escape.

Walk in a counterclockwise (widdershins) circle around the room, chanting:

"Turn and turn about, out, out, out,
Badness put to rout, end to every doubt,
Out, out, out."

As you chant, use your hands to 'sweep' the hurtful emotions out the window, visualizing them leaving your space.

Place ylang-ylang, myrrh, and coriander essential oils in an oil burner and light it.

Walk in a clockwise (deosil) circle around the room, chanting:

"Winding, winding, winding,
Peace and joy now finding,
A love that's true and binding,
Winding, winding, winding."

Continue to walk and chant until you feel the energy in the room shift to one of peace and harmony.

Close the window, sealing in the positive energy and ensuring the jealousy has been banished.

"As I will, so let it be,
Jealousy banished, love now free."

Basil and Cinnamon Love Talisman

REQUIREMENTS:

❊ A large, flat plate
❊ A small picture of yourself (no one else should be in it)
❊ Ground cinnamon
❊ Dried basil
❊ A ceramic bowl
❊ A pink candle
❊ A candle holder
❊ A small piece of pink cotton cloth
❊ Pink yarn
❊ Matches
❊ A heat-proof container for the spent matches

INSTRUCTIONS:

Hold the pink candle between your hands.

Close your eyes and envision yourself as a loving person, filled with love and light.

Infuse the candle with this loving energy.

Place the candle in its holder and light it.

Place the plate before the candle.

Put the small picture of yourself in the middle of the plate.

Using a spoon or the bottle of cinnamon, create a small circle of ground cinnamon around the picture, chanting:

> "By this spice, my heart is true,
> Love now finds its way to you."

Pour a larger circle of dried basil around the cinnamon ring, chanting once more:

> "Herbs of Earth, my call you heed,
> Bring forth the love that I need."

Finally, pour a third, larger circle of ground cinnamon around the basil circle, chanting again:

> "With this charm, my wish I send,
> A love that's pure, on me depend."

Hold your hands, palms down, over the three herb circles and your picture.

Feel the energies rising from the herbs and raise your own energy.

Visualize love surrounding you and flowing into the herbs.

Carefully pour the herbs and the picture into the ceramic bowl.

Place your hands into the bowl and mix the herbs with your fingers, sending energy into them, while saying these or similar words:

> "Spice and herb, plant and tree,
> Send someone to love me.
> Love we'll share equally,
> As I will, so shall it be!"

Dust off your hands.

Pour the spices and the picture into the center of the pink cloth.

Gather up the ends, twist them together, and tie them shut with the pink yarn.

Place the love talisman beside the candle. Let it sit there for at least 18 minutes.

Afterward, pinch out the candle's flame (or snuff it) and carry the talisman with you to attract love.

Burn the candle at approximately the same time each day for at least 7 minutes.

Love will find you.

You should make another one in about 7 months.

Bring Back a Lover

REQUIREMENTS:

❁ Two white candles
❁ A photo or drawing of your lover or friend (alone)
❁ A photo of yourself smiling
❁ A chamomile tea bag
❁ A piece of blue material

INSTRUCTIONS:

At exactly **8:00** in the evening, light the candles and take deep breaths to relax.

Visualize a serene, beautiful scene.

Hold the picture of the person and say:

"By the light of the flame,
Your desire I proclaim.
When I speak your name,
Our hearts are the same."

Say their name slowly three times, then place your picture face down on theirs.

Wrap the two pictures and the tea bag in the blue cloth.

Store the package in a safe place.

To ensure your message reaches them, light the candles at **8:00** each night and say their name three times.

After three weeks, suggest meeting for lunch or dinner.

Bring Someone Close

REQUIREMENTS:

✤ Full Moon Water
✤ Photos of you and your beloved
✤ A candle
✤ A bowl of water
✤ Come To Me oil (optional)
✤ Come To Me incense (optional)

INSTRUCTIONS:

Place the photos of you and your beloved side by side.

Light the Come To Me incense, allowing its fragrance to fill the space.

Drip Full Moon Water over the photos, visualizing your beloved coming closer with each drop.

Chant:

"Sacred water flow from me,
Draw him near, so mote it be."

Anoint a candle with Come To Me oil, if using.

Set the candle in a bowl of water and light it, letting it burn until the water extinguishes the flame.

Visualize your beloved finding their way to you, feeling the pull of your love.

Chant:

"As endless rivers run to sea,
His path to me is clear, and free."

Envision your beloved arriving, their heart filled with the certainty of your love.

Chant:

> "A love that's true, once here he'll find,
> Our lives to blend, in heart and mind."

Chant to Seal the Spell:

> "Water blessed by moon's fair light,
> Draw my love, both day and night.
> In his heart and soul, he'll see,
> Our destined love, so mote it be."

Chinese Love Talisman

REQUIREMENTS:

✿ A red candle
✿ Rose petals
✿ A small piece of parchment
✿ A quill and red ink
✿ Incense of your choice

INSTRUCTIONS:

Cleanse the area with incense. Light the red candle, symbolizing passionate love.

On the piece of parchment, write the name of the woman whose love you seek with the quill and red ink.

Sprinkle rose petals around the candle. Place the parchment beneath the candle. Chant:

"With Love's powerful arrow, I pierce thy heart,
O woman, let passion and desire start.
Love that causes unease, burning bright,
Draws you to me, by magick's might.
The arrow, flying true and straight,
Brings burning desire, seals our fate.
Its point is love, its shaft, my will,
Thy heart is pierced, thy love fulfilled.
Reluctance fades, thy pride takes flight,
Come to me now, this very night.
Thy mother, thy father, none shall prevent,
Thy heart is mine, with love's intent.
O Mitra, O Varuna, strip her willpower,
I wield the power, in this sacred hour.
I alone hold sway over her heart,
Bound by love, we shall not part."

28

Meditate on your love for her, visualizing her heart opening to you. Feel the energy of the spell flowing through you and into the candle.

Allow the candle to burn down completely, melting the wax over the parchment. Once the candle has burned out, keep the wax-covered parchment as a talisman.

Stand in gratitude and say:

"By the power of Mitra and Varuna, by love's eternal flame, this spell is sealed, our hearts aflame."

Keep the talisman close to you until you see the desired results. Store it in a safe place, treating it with respect and reverence.

Daisies of Love

REQUIREMENTS:

❀ Twenty-one bright yellow daisies
❀ A water-filled vase
❀ One pink candle
❀ Powdered coriander

INSTRUCTIONS:

Gather your daisies, vase, candle, and coriander. Find a quiet, serene space to perform the spell.

Place the vase filled with water before you. Focus your intention on attracting a virtuous and honest lover. Whisper to the water:

"Water, pure and true, bring forth a faithful love to me."

Position the pink candle, symbolizing your future lover, in front of the vase. Light the candle, letting its flame represent the purity and passion of your desire.

Arrange seven daisies in the vase, saying:

"Daisies bright, love's pure delight,
bring honesty to me this night."

Remove the petals from seven more daisies, and scatter them around the vase and candle, chanting:

"Petals fall, love's true call,
honesty surround us all."

Place the last seven daisies flat in front of you. Sprinkle the powdered coriander over all the flowers, intoning:

"Coriander's spice, love's sweet entice,
bring virtue and honesty, pure and precise."

Walk seven blocks from your home, carrying the final daisy. As you drop one daisy at each block, say:

"Maiden, Mother, and Crone,
bless my love and make it known.
Break all curses, set me free,
by the power of three times three."

Stand before the final daisy, heart open and sincere:

"Aphrodite, Goddess fair,
hear my plea, my heart lay bare.
Forgive my wrongs, guide my way,
bless my love, I humbly pray.
By your grace, let love renew,
honest, faithful, pure, and true."

Pour out your heart, confessing any past misdeeds and vowing to honor love's gifts:

"I vow to shower love with care,
be faithful, honest, always fair.
No empty promise, no deceit,
with love and truth my heart will beat.
Aphrodite, hear my plea,
bless this love eternally."

As you walk back home, feel the energy of Aphrodite surrounding you, guiding you towards true love. Trust in her power, and know that your sincere heart will attract the love you seek.

Dual Candle Love Spell

INSTRUCTIONS:

✿ 2 candles: One white and one in your favorite color
✿ 2 candle holders
✿ A rose-colored altar cloth
✿ A piece of red chalk

SPELL INSTRUCTIONS:

In the sacred circle, ground yourself and center your energy.

Lay out the rose-colored altar cloth and place the candles in their holders.

Meditate deeply on any preconceived ideas you have about the perfect partner.

Release these notions, understanding that clinging to superficial attributes may blind you to your true ideal mate.

When your mind is clear and open, hold the candle of your favorite color, representing yourself.

Meditate on the qualities and energies you bring to a relationship. Speak these aloud:

> *"I offer love, compassion, and trust,*
> *In a bond that's pure and just.*
> *I bring strength, joy, and light,*
> *To share my heart, both day and night."*

Place your candle back on the altar and pick up the white candle, representing your ideal partner.

Speak aloud the essential qualities you desire in a mate, asking Aphrodite to unite you in this lifetime:

"Aphrodite, goddess of love so fair,
Hear my plea and answer this prayer.
Bring forth a partner true and kind,
A loving soul, in heart and mind."

Place the two candles in their holders at opposite ends of the altar.

Draw a heart in the center of the altar with the red chalk, large enough for both candle holders to fit inside.

Each day, meditate for a few minutes on the perfect loving relationship.

Move the two candles an inch closer together daily.

If you start on the new moon, by the full moon the candles should be touching in the center of the heart.

When they meet, draw two more hearts around the first one.

Raise energy by singing your favorite love song, infusing the candles with your desires:

"Hearts entwined, spirits bright,
Love's pure magic, day and night.
Candles joined, our love shall be,
By Aphrodite's grace, so mote it be!"

Enchant a Ring for Marriage

REQUIREMENTS:

❁ A gold-colored ring
❁ Red wine
❁ Water
❁ One oak leaf
❁ One willow leaf
❁ One bay leaf
❁ Two blades of grass
❁ A piece of silver paper
❁ A vessel or jar
❁ A string or cord

INSTRUCTIONS:

Choose a gold-colored ring that fits your wedding finger well.

Fill a vessel halfway with red wine and the other half with water.

Add one oak leaf, one willow leaf, one bay leaf, and two blades of grass to the vessel.

Write the name of your beloved on a piece of silver paper and place it in the vessel.

Cover the vessel tightly and place it near a window where it can catch the sun's rays.

Leave it there from the crescent moon until the full moon.

On the night of the full moon, retrieve the vessel and take out the ring.

Hold the ring in your hands, close your eyes, and focus on your beloved.

While rubbing the ring, recite the following words three times:

"Ring of gold, in wine and leaf,
Bind our hearts beyond belief.
With oak, and willow, bay, and grass,
Seal this love that none surpass.
With moon's bright light and sun's warm ray,
Draw my love to me, I pray.
Keep this secret, name concealed,
Until our bond in truth is sealed."

Wear the ring hidden on a string around your neck.

Do not reveal the name of your beloved until your wish has come true.

Keep the ring close and wear it until your desire is fulfilled. Treat it with reverence and secrecy, allowing its magic to work.

Enchantment for a Joyous Union

REQUIREMENTS:

❁ 6 stalks of fresh lavender
❁ 1 rubber band
❁ 1 yard of pink ribbon
❁ 1 yard of burgundy ribbon

INSTRUCTIONS:

Gather the lavender stalks together and secure their ends with the rubber band.

Braid the lavender stalks using two stalks per strand, envisioning a blissful and harmonious life with your spouse.

As you braid, recite:

> "Bless this union, pure and bright,
> Husband and wife, bound in light."

When nearing the flowered ends of the braid, center the pink and burgundy ribbons.

Securely tie the braid with the ribbons, then criss-cross them around the braid, working back toward the end.

As you wrap the ribbon around the braid, chant:

> "Two hearts united, bound as one,
> Joy and love, till life is done."

Tie the ribbons in a bow near the stalk ends.

Hang the charm above the bed or in a special place within the bedroom.

This charm can also be given as a heartfelt wedding gift. Instruct the recipients to hang it in their bedroom to bless their union.

Final Blessing:

"By lavender's scent and ribbon's grace,
May love and joy fill this space.
Two lives entwined, forever blessed,
In happiness, may they rest."

Enchanted Love Sachet

REQUIREMENTS:

❀ 3 parts Rose petals
❀ 2 parts Orange blossoms
❀ 1 part Jasmine flowers
❀ 1 part Gardenia flowers
❀ A small sachet bag (preferably pink or red)

INSTRUCTIONS:

Collect the rose petals, orange blossoms, jasmine flowers, and gardenia flowers.

Lay them out under the light of a waxing moon to absorb its energy, visualizing love and harmony filling each petal.

Mix the flower petals together in a bowl, combining their energies.

As you blend the petals, chant:

> "Petals of rose, orange, jasmine, and gardenia,
> Unite your power, bring love's euphoria."

Fill the small sachet bag with the enchanted flower mixture.

Seal the bag tightly, visualizing it glowing with the energy of love and attraction.

Hold the sachet close to your heart and say:

> "With flowers fair, I weave this charm,
> To bring me love, tender and warm.
> By moonlit night and daylight bright,
> Love's embrace, pure and light."

Final Blessing:

"Flower's scent and moon's soft light,
Bring forth love, true and bright.
With heart sincere and spirit free,
Love shall come, blessed by thee."

Keep the sachet under your pillow, in your drawer, or carry it with you to attract love and positive relationships into your life.

Enchantment of the Loving Bell

This magical bell, carried by the winds, will send forth your yearning for love, drawing to you a companion who listens and responds to your heart's call.

REQUIREMENTS:

❀ A small bell with a pleasant ring

INSTRUCTIONS:

Find a window frequently open, through which the West wind blows.

Hang the bell in this window, ensuring it catches the breeze.

With the bell in place, speak these words with heartfelt intent:

> "Bell of love, with gentle sound,
> Whisper my need, let it be found.
> On Westward winds, my call you send,
> Draw to me a loving friend.
> Bell of love, with voice so clear,
> Speak to your kin, bring my love near."

As the bell sways and rings, imagine it sending out your desire for love into the world.

Envision the sound reaching other bells, amplifying your call for a loving companion.

Whisper softly:

> "With every chime, my heart does yearn,
> Bring love to me, for which I burn.
> By bell's sweet song and winds that blow,
> My true love, to me, you'll show."

Every time the bell rings, know it is carrying your desire for love to the winds.

Trust that the other bells will hear and amplify your call, guiding your true love to you.

Enchantment of True Love

REQUIREMENTS:

❀ Seven small stones
❀ A handful of rose petals
❀ Apple seeds
❀ A lodestone

INSTRUCTIONS:

Gather the seven small stones and place them in a circle on your altar or a sacred space.

In the center of the circle, scatter the rose petals and apple seeds.

Place the lodestone directly in the middle of the circle, atop the rose petals and apple seeds.

Stand before the circle, close your eyes, and focus on your intention to attract true love.

Chant the following incantation with passion and belief:

> "Petals of rose and seeds of apple,
> With stones encircle, magic grapple.
> Lodestone mighty, draw with might,
> Perfect love to me, by moon's bright light.
> Dragon's mist and night's soft breath,
> Bring love to me, beyond life's death.
> From the cosmos, true love draw,
> By ancient power, this sacred law."

Visualize the energy from the stones, petals, seeds, and lodestone combining and radiating out into the universe, drawing love towards you.

Leave the circle undisturbed overnight or until you feel the energy has fully manifested.

Once complete, gather the stones, petals, seeds, and lodestone and keep them in a special place or bury them in your garden to seal the spell.

Enflame Desire

REQUIREMENTS:

✹ 3 hairs from the head of your desired one
✹ A candle in the shape of a phallus (for a man) or a womb (for a woman), red for passion or green for love
✹ Olive oil
✹ A plain piece of paper

INSTRUCTIONS:

If crafting your own candle, do so on a Friday, embedding the three hairs into the soft wax as you mold it.

If using a pre-made candle, gently soften the wax with a lighter and press the hairs into it.

On a Friday night, under a waxing moon, take the candle into your hands.

Focus intently on the relationship you desire with your loved one. Visualize yourselves together, experiencing all the passion and affection you crave.

Anoint the candle with olive oil, caressing it as though you are tending to your lover. Maintain your visualization throughout this process.

Light the candle, invoking the essence of your desired love.

Write your lover's name three times on the piece of paper.

Burn the paper in the candle's flame, chanting your lover's name aloud three times as it burns.

Extinguish the candle gently.

Chant:

"Wax and flame, desire ignite,
Bring my love to me tonight.
(Name of lover), hear my plea,
Come to me, so shall it be."

Ensure Faithful Love

REQUIREMENTS:

❋ Senna Pods
❋ Powdered liquorice
❋ Linden
❋ Marigolds or rosemary
❋ Cumin

INSTRUCTIONS:

Brew tea from the senna pods.

Strain and pour the liquid into the bathwater of your lover without their knowledge.

As you pour, whisper:

"With this brew, fidelity grows,
Bound by love, true heart shows."

Sprinkle powdered liquorice over the footprints of your lover.

Chant softly:

"By this trace, love stays in place,
True and steadfast, with gentle grace."

Moisten a small amount of linden on the palm of your right hand.

Dab it on your lover's forehead while they sleep, murmuring:

"In dreams, in light, faithful heart take flight,
Bound by linden, true love's sight."

Place a handful of marigolds or rosemary in, around, and underneath the bed where your lover sleeps.

As you do, chant:

> "Marigold bright, rosemary's might,
> Guard this bed, keep love in sight."

Mix cumin into your lover's food or drink, especially if you are to be separated.

Whisper with intent:

> "Cumin's power, in meal or flower,
> Keeps love faithful, hour by hour."

Stand before the prepared items, visualizing your lover's unwavering devotion.

Recite:

> "Herbs of magic, pure and true,
> Bind my love, no heart anew.
> By earth and water, fire and air,
> This spell is cast with loving care."

Hasten a Marriage

REQUIREMENTS:

❀ Two dolls dressed as bride and groom
❀ A yard of white ribbon
❀ Valerian
❀ Benzoin
❀ Cinnamon
❀ Myrrh
❀ Holy Water
❀ Honey
❀ A lodestone
❀ A length of vine
❀ A shoebox

INSTRUCTIONS:

On the backs of the dolls, inscribe the names of the man and woman who are to be wed.

Write their names on the white ribbon as well.

Make three knots in the ribbon, each time asking the spirits for their assistance in hastening the marriage.

> "Spirits of love, hear my plea,
> Knot by knot, bring them to be."

Bind the dolls together at the waist, face to face, using the knotted ribbon.

In a bowl or bucket, create an herbal 'tea' with valerian, benzoin, cinnamon, and myrrh.

Submerge the bound dolls in the liquid.

Recite three Hail Marys and three Our Fathers as the dolls soak in the herbal mixture.

> "Hail Mary, full of grace,
> Bless this union in Your embrace."

Remove the dolls from the liquid, sprinkle them with Holy Water, and place them in a shoebox.

Wash the lodestone with honey and Holy Water, then add it to the box along with the length of vine.

Place the shoebox in a safe place where it will remain undisturbed.

Speak these final words to seal the spell:

> "Holy spirits, guide their way,
> Bring forth the wedding day.
> With love and grace, let it be,
> As I will, so shall it be."

Keep the shoebox secure, and trust in the power of the spell to hasten the blessed union.

Invoke Sweet Thoughts in Another

REQUIREMENTS:

❀ A clean bottle with a tight cap
❀ A used Popsicle stick (consume the Popsicle, any flavor)
❀ Honey
❀ Red thread
❀ A small lock of your loved one's hair

INSTRUCTIONS:

Enjoy a delicious Popsicle, savoring each bite. Keep the stick once finished.

Tie a piece of red thread around the lock of your loved one's hair.

Place the Popsicle stick into the bottle, symbolizing your lips and the connection you seek.

Add the lock of hair tied with red thread into the bottle.

Pour honey into the bottle, letting it fill completely. As you do, envision the sweetness of love and the warm thoughts you wish to invoke.

Cap the bottle tightly, sealing the magic within.

Hold the bottle in your hands and chant:

"Honey sweet, with love so bright,
Bind his/her thoughts, day and night.
By my lips and love so true,
Think of me in all you do."

Each time you turn the bottle upside down, imagine your loved one's thoughts sweetening towards you.

Chant:

> "With every turn, may sweet thoughts flow,
> In their heart, my love shall grow.
> By the power of honey and red thread,
> Our love and thoughts are gently spread."

As you finish, say:

> "As I will, so shall it be,
> Sweet thoughts of love, sent by me."

Keep this enchanted bottle in a special place, turning it whenever you wish to remind your loved one of your sweetness.

Key to the Heart

REQUIREMENTS:

❁ A found key (preferably an antique)
❁ Your pure intent and love
❁ A safe place to keep the key

INSTRUCTIONS:

Reflect on your love for the person you desire. Visualize the two of you together, sharing a deep and lasting bond.

When you find the key, say the following incantation:

"The key to your heart lies on the ground,
The key to your heart has now been found.
I lock up your love with the heart of my own,
I'll guard it forever with the love I have shown."

Hold the key in your hand, close your eyes, and focus on the feelings of love and protection you have for your beloved. Envision the key glowing with the power of your intent.

For nine consecutive nights, sleep with the key under your pillow, allowing it to absorb your dreams and desires for a harmonious relationship.

Carry the key with you during the day, keeping it close to your heart. Each time you touch it, reaffirm your love and visualize the bond strengthening between you and your beloved.

After the ninth night, place the key in a safe and special place, where it will continue to guard and nurture your love.

Conclude with this chant to seal the spell and affirm your intent:

"With this key, our love I bind,
Hearts entwined, in love we find.
Guardian of love, strong and true,
This key protects both me and you."

Trust in the magic you have woven, and let the key safeguard your love eternally.

Kissing Spell

REQUIREMENTS:

❀ Red lipstick
❀ White paper
❀ Red candle

INSTRUCTIONS:

Take the red lipstick and draw a lip print on a piece of white paper.

Light the red candle, letting its flame illuminate your intentions.

Hold the paper with the lip print close to the candle flame.

Visualize the person you desire, focusing on their lips meeting yours.

As you burn the paper, chant:

> "Kiss me when we meet, Kiss me, (Full Name), so sweet.
> Greet me with your lips, divine,
> Say you missed me, intertwine.
> Most of all, just kiss me true,
> Let our love and passion brew."

Continue to visualize the person kissing you, feeling the warmth and connection.

Conjure love and passion in your heart, letting the magic flow.

Allow the paper to burn completely, knowing that your intention has been set into the universe. The power of belief and magic will guide the outcome, drawing the person closer to you.

Embrace the magic within, and let the spell weave its enchantment.

<u>NOTES</u>

Lavender Love Letter

REQUIREMENTS:

❀ A sheet of stationery
❀ Lavender sprigs or lavender oil
❀ Dove's blood ink (or red ink as an alternative)
❀ A quill or pen

INSTRUCTIONS:

Gently rub the entire sheet of stationery with lavender sprigs or dab a few drops of lavender oil on it.

As you do this, envision your words being infused with enchantment and allure.

Use Dove's blood ink if available. If not, substitute with red ink. Focus on the ink being a conduit for your heartfelt emotions and intentions.

Sit in a quiet, magical space where you can concentrate.

Write your love letter, pouring your true feelings and desires into every word. Visualize the recipient being irresistibly drawn to your words and the emotions they convey.

Once you have finished writing, hold the letter in your hands, close your eyes, and chant:

> "By lavender's scent and ink of dove,
> I bind this letter with magical love.
> May my words enchant and allure,
> Drawing you in, forevermore.
> With every stroke, my heart's decree,
> Come to me, so mote it be."

Fold the letter carefully, sealing it with a kiss if you wish.

Send or deliver the letter to the recipient, knowing that the enchantment will guide their response.

Chant:

> By lavender's charm and ink's delight,
> This spell is cast, by day or night.
> As I have written, so shall it be,
> Love's true magic, come to me.

Love Knots

REQUIREMENTS:

❀ Three cords or strings of pastel colors (e.g., pink, red, and lilac)

INSTRUCTIONS:

Gather three cords or strings of pastel colors such as pink, red, and lilac. Braid the cords together, infusing them with your intent.

Firmly tie a knot near one end of the braid, focusing on your need for love.

Chant as you tie each knot: "By knot of one, love has begun."

Tie the second knot, saying: "By knot of two, love comes through."

Continue tying knots and chanting until you have tied seven knots in total.

Complete Chant:

> By knot of one, love has begun,
> By knot of two, love comes through,
> By knot of three, love to me,
> By knot of four, love will soar,
> By knot of five, love arrives,
> By knot of six, love we fix,
> By knot of seven, love is given."

Chant to Seal the Spell:

"Knots of love, bind so tight,
Draw to me love's pure light.
By this cord, love is found,
In sacred space, love is bound."

Wear or carry the cord with you until you find your love, letting it draw love to you.

Once love has found you, keep the cord in a safe place or offer it to one of the elements.

If you choose to release it, burn the cord and toss the ashes into a stream, saying:

"Love fulfilled, set free,
By earth, air, fire, and sea."

Make Yourself Known to Another

REQUIREMENTS:

❀ Soil from your beloved's footprint
❀ A willow tree
❀ A small trowel or digging tool

INSTRUCTIONS:

Find the footprint of your beloved in the earth. Carefully dig up the soil where their footprint is, collecting it in a small container.

Find a willow tree, known for its associations with love and emotion. Bring the soil from the footprint with you.

At the base of the willow tree, use your trowel to dig a small hole. As you work, visualize the connection between you and your beloved growing stronger.

As you place the soil from the footprint into the hole, speak these words with intent and focus:

> "Many earths on earth there be,
> I make my love known unto thee.
> For he is the flower and I the stem,
> He the cock and I the hen.
> Grow, grow, O willow tree,
> Sorrow not for the likes of me."

Cover the footprint soil with the earth from the willow tree, sealing your intention. Visualize the roots of the willow tree intertwining with the essence of your beloved, drawing their attention to you.

Sit quietly for a moment, focusing on your desire to be noticed. Feel the magic working through the earth, the willow, and the connection you've created.

Give thanks to the willow tree for its assistance. You may leave a small offering such as a coin or a piece of ribbon tied around a branch as a token of gratitude.

"With earth and tree, my love I send,
A connection made, a heart to mend.
Eyes will open, hearts will see,
As I wish, so shall it be."

Leave the area with confidence, knowing that your spell is working to bring you to the attention of your beloved.

Overcome Relationship Troubles

When things get tough and you need to resolve issues in your relationship, this is a hidden source of inspiration.

REQUIREMENTS:

❀ A pink candle
❀ Love oil (such as rose or jasmine)
❀ Herbs associated with love (like rosemary or lavender)

INSTRUCTIONS:

Hold the pink candle in your hands.

Close your eyes and visualize you and your lover in a happy, loving embrace.

Pour the energy from this vision into the candle, imagining it filling with warm, glowing light.

With heartfelt intention, say aloud:

> *"By the Goddess and God above,*
> *We will always share our love.*
> *In times of joy and times of strife,*
> *May love remain within our life."*

On a Friday during a waxing moon, take out the candle.

Apply a few drops of love oil to your index finger.

Starting from the center of the candle, anoint upwards to the wick, then from the center down to the base.

Light the candle and let it burn completely until it extinguishes itself.

As the candle burns, focus on its flame, visualizing it strengthening the bond and love between you and your partner.

Sit by the candlelight, meditating on the positive energy and love being reinforced by the flame.

Allow yourself to feel the warmth and comfort of this magical act.

Chant:

"Oils of love, herbs of might,
Strengthen our bond, keep it tight.
Flame of passion, burn so bright,
Guide us through each rocky night."

Keep the candle hidden and safe for future use whenever you feel the need to reinforce your relationship's bond and confidence in your love.

Pink Cloth Love Spell

REQUIREMENTS:

❁ A lighter
❁ A pink candle
❁ Musk oil
❁ A pin
❁ Marjoram herb
❁ A small pink cloth with "dream of me, be with me" on one side and "just a little nudge" on the other
❁ A small pink or red pouch
❁ A metal or glass plate

INSTRUCTIONS:

Cast your circle and call the quarters as usual.

Dim the lights, leaving a single candle burning if desired.

Take the pink candle and anoint it with musk oil while thinking of your intended.

With the pin, scratch the name of the person on one side of the candle and the word "love" on the other.

Place the pink cloth on the plate with "just a little nudge" facing down.

Chant:

"Dream of me,
be with me,
With this nudge,
let our love be free."

Light the pink candle.

Affix the cloth to the plate by letting hot wax drip on the corners of the cloth.

While visualizing your desire, use the wax drippings to form the shape of a heart in the middle of the cloth.

Drip some wax in the center of the heart and place the candle there.

With the candle burning, empower a pinch of marjoram by pinching it tightly between your fingers, feeling the energy flowing into it.

Sprinkle the marjoram on the plate, touching the heart and candle.

Let the candle burn down completely.

Crinkle the hardened pool of wax as much as you can while thinking of your desire.

Take the remains of the wax, marjoram, and the cloth and place them in the small pink or red pouch.

Sleep with the pouch under your pillow, using dream direction to focus on the intended person. Even if you don't remember the dream, trust that the magic is working.

Continue this nightly until the day you are going to meet the person.

On the day you meet the person, carry the pouch with you.

When the moment feels right, close your eyes and touch the pouch, feeling its power.

Open your eyes and look directly at the intended, channeling your desire.

Chant to Seal the Spell:

With this pouch, our paths align, Love's true power, now is mine. So mote it be!

Reconciliation

REQUIREMENTS:

- ❀ 1 white candle
- ❀ 1 blue candle
- ❀ 1 pink candle
- ❀ Love oil for anointing the candles

INSTRUCTIONS:

Cleanse your ritual area, ensuring it's free from negativity. Arrange your candles and have your love oil ready.

Anoint each candle with the love oil. As you do so, focus on your intention of reconciliation and peace. Carve your name and the name of the person you wish to reconcile with into the blue candle.

Create a protective circle around your space, invoking Cerridwen and Pan for their guidance and blessings.

Light the white candle first, saying:

"Cerridwen, Mother, hear my plea,
Bless this flame to remove hostility."

Light the blue candle next, saying:

"Mother and Father, hear my call,
Between [Name] and I, let tranquility fall."

Light the pink candle last, saying:

"Pan and Eros, blessed be,
If love remains, let it shine brightly.
For the good of all and harm to none,
Our hearts entwined, the spell is done."

Sit quietly, focusing on the flames of the candles. Visualize peace and love flowing between you and the person you wish to reconcile with. Feel the warmth of reconciliation filling your heart.

Close your circle, thanking Cerridwen and Pan for their assistance. Allow the candles to burn down completely.

Final Blessing:

"By the light of these flames, our bond renew,
With love and peace, we start anew.
Harmony restored, our hearts set free,
As I wish, so shall it be."

Keep any remnants of the candles in a safe place as a reminder of your intention and the magic that was cast.

Rekindle Passion Between Lovers

REQUIREMENTS:

❀ A fully blooming rose
❀ Two pieces of pink or red cloth (preferably silk or linen)

Timing: This spell works best just before a full moon or when the moon is in Libra.

INSTRUCTIONS:

Hold the rose in your hands, feeling its energy and beauty.

Chant the following incantation, filling it with your intention:

"Lovers, [Your Name] and [Lover's Name], side by side,
Passion and desire, our hearts and loins provide.
May this night be one of great delight,
Under moon's soft glow, we reignite."

Gently scatter the rose petals across your bed.

Sleep with your lover amidst the petals, allowing their fragrance and energy to enhance your connection.

Make passionate love, focusing on rekindling your bond and excitement.

The next morning, gather the petals together.

Place them into two pieces of pink or red cloth, one for each of you.

Tie the cloths securely, creating two small sachets.

Place each sachet under each one's pillow.

These sachets will serve as a continuous charm to keep the passion alive in your relationship.

As you finish, envision the love and passion between you and your partner growing stronger.

Whisper a final blessing:

> "By rose's bloom and moon's light,
> Our passion reignited, burning bright.
> Love and desire, intertwined as one,
> Our hearts and bodies, forever spun."

Keep these sachets under your pillows to maintain the magic, and let the rekindled passion strengthen your bond.

Release an Ex-Lover

REQUIREMENTS:

❊ A photo of you and your ex-lover from a happy time
❊ Scissors
❊ A fireproof dish or cauldron
❊ A candle (white or black)
❊ A small shovel or trowel

INSTRUCTIONS:

Cast a sacred circle to create your magical space.

Carefully cut out your ex-lover's image from the photo, separating it from yours.

Light the candle and place it near your working area, allowing its light to guide your release.

Hold the cut-out image of your ex-lover over the flame, then place it in the fireproof dish or cauldron to burn. As it burns, recite:

"Flame of release, consume this past,
Letting go, my heart beats fast.
Joyful future now I see,
Free from the bonds that once held me."

Envision a hopeful and joyful life without this person. Focus on your happiness, freedom, and the new opportunities that await you. Do not harbor any blame or thoughts of revenge; instead, fill your heart with peace and acceptance.

Once the image is reduced to ashes, take them outside to an appropriate place. Using the shovel or trowel, bury the ashes in the earth, symbolizing your release. As you do so, say:

"Ashes to earth, the past is gone,
I embrace the future, bright as dawn.
With this act, I am free,
My heart is open, so let it be."

Close the circle, thanking any deities or spirits you invoked for their assistance.

Feel the weight lift from your shoulders as you release the past and embrace a future filled with possibilities and joy.

Release Unwanted Romantic Feelings

REQUIREMENTS:

❀ A small slip of paper
❀ Pen
❀ A quiet, reflective space
❀ A small spade or trowel

Note:

Perform this spell under a waning moon for best results, as this phase is ideal for banishing and letting go.

INSTRUCTIONS:

Find a quiet place where you can focus without interruption.

Reflect deeply on the person from whom you wish to release your romantic feelings. Consider all the reasons and traits that support your decision.

Write the person's name on the small slip of paper.

With deliberate intent, cross out their name.

As you cross out the name, chant the following words with conviction:

"You no longer hold a place in my heart,
You are not the one for me,
I release these feelings, it's time to part,
From this bond, I now set free."

Under the light of the waning moon, take the paper outside.

Dig a small hole in the ground.

Bury the paper, along with all your feelings for this person.

As you cover the paper with earth, chant:

> "I bury these feelings deep in the ground,
> With the waning moon, they are bound,
> New beginnings await, fresh and clear,
> My heart is free, my mind sincere."

Pat the earth gently and take a moment to feel the release.

Walk away without looking back, knowing that you have made a fresh start.

Reveal Hidden Love

Requirements:

- One pink candle
- A carving tool (such as a pin or knife)
- A quiet, undisturbed space

Instructions:

Carve six evenly spaced rings around the pink candle, creating seven equal sections.

Find a quiet place where you won't be disturbed. Light the pink candle and focus on the person you believe loves you but hesitates to confess.

With the candle lit, call upon the name of the one you desire and say:

"Gana, be with me in all I do,
Gana, bring forth a love that's true.
Grant him (her) courage to voice their heart,
Let their love for me now start."

Spend a few moments imagining the person coming to you, expressing their love openly and sincerely.

Repeat the chant while focusing on the candle flame:

"Gana, be with me in all I do,
Gana, bring forth a love that's true.
Grant him (her) courage to voice their heart,
Let their love for me now start."

Continue this until the candle burns down to the first carved ring. Then, extinguish the flame by pinching it out (never blow it out).

Repeat this ritual at the same hour every Friday for seven weeks, each time burning down to the next ring.

On the seventh week, continue until the candle burns itself out completely.

Chant:

> By the light of the pink candle's glow,
> Reveal the love that needs to show.
> If their heart is true, let them speak,
> Courage and love are what they seek.

Rosehips to Attract Desire

REQUIREMENTS:

✿ Essence or extract of rose hips

INSTRUCTIONS:

Hold the bottle of rose hip essence in your hands and close your eyes.

Visualize yourself radiating allure and magnetism, attracting the desire and attention you seek.

Just before you go out, place two drops of the rose hip essence on one wrist.

Rub your wrists together briskly to spread the essence.

As you rub your wrists together, chant softly:

> "Rose hips red, essence of desire,
> Ignite the spark, set hearts afire.
> By this charm, attraction's bloom,
> Draw their gaze within this room."

Carry the bottle with you to refresh the essence if needed. A few drops on your wrists will ensure the charm remains potent throughout the day or night.

Note:

This charm is designed to work at close range, so you may need to reapply it if you plan to be out for extended periods. The power of rose hips will help you get noticed and flirted with, especially by males.

Soulmates' Fiery Love

REQUIREMENTS:

❀ A charred stick
❀ Dried rose petals
❀ A piece of paper
❀ A red candle
❀ A heat-proof container

INSTRUCTIONS:

Take the charred stick and use it as a pencil to draw two interlinked hearts on the paper. As you draw, visualize yourself in a fulfilling and passionate relationship. Draw with intention and power.

Hold the dried rose petals in your projective hand. Channel fiery, loving energies into the petals, imagining them glowing with vibrant energy.

Sprinkle the charged rose petals over the interlinked hearts on the paper. Visualize the petals infusing the hearts with love and passion.

Carefully wrap the paper around the rose petals, creating a small package. Continue to focus on your visualization of a passionate relationship.

Light the red candle. Hold the package in the flame until it catches fire, then place it into a heat-proof container. As it burns, chant with conviction:

"Fiery hearts, intertwined,
Passion's flame, now combined.
Love's desire, strong and true,
Bring my soulmate into view."

Watch the package burn completely, visualizing the release of your spell's energy into the universe. Feel the power of the spell working to bring your love to you.

Roses Effigy Ritual

Requirements:

- A dozen roses
- A large candle (preferably human-shaped in the correct gender) with the person's name written or carved on it
- A photograph of the person or a piece of paper with their name written on it
- A tray

Timing: During the waxing moon

Instructions:

Place the photograph or the piece of paper with the person's name in the center of the tray.

Set the candle on top of the photograph or paper.

Arrange the dozen roses around the candle on the tray.

Hold the candle in your hands and say with conviction:

"Candle, I name you [Person's Name]."

Believe deeply as you speak, for your belief empowers the spell.

Place the candle back atop the photograph or paper and light it.

As the candle burns, repeat the incantation, focusing on your desire and ensuring safety to prevent any fire hazards.

Repeat the following as the candle melts:

"I melt your heart as I melt this wax,
Even as this wax flows,
So your love glows for me.
I melt your heart as I melt this wax,
Even as this wax flows,
So your love flows to me.
I melt your heart as I melt this wax,
Even as this wax flows,
So your love grows for me.
I melt your heart as I melt this wax,
And by its molten flow,
Your love for me will show."

Allow the candle to burn down completely, focusing on your intention throughout.

Once the candle has melted and the wax has cooled, scrape up the wax-encrusted photograph or paper.

Gather the roses, tie them together, and hang them upside down to dry.

Keep the wax-encrusted photograph or paper and the dried roses in a secret place until the spell has manifested.

Note:

The roses serve as an offering to the Love Goddess. Ensure to use a full dozen to honor her properly.

Strengthen Love's Bond

REQUIREMENTS:

�֎ Two ribbons (pink or red, each 8-12 inches long)
✖ Usual ritual tools for opening the Magic Circle

INSTRUCTIONS:

Ensure your intentions are pure and true. This spell is for strengthening an existing relationship, not for coercing someone against their will.

Begin by opening the Magic Circle as you usually do.

The couple kneels before the altar, hands clasped together.

The lady begins the invocation, with her partner repeating each line, or they may speak in unison:

> "Goddess of love, so fair and bright,
> Bless us here in your sacred light.
> God of strength, with power so true,
> Grant your blessing on us two."

They turn to face each other. The man leads, followed by the lady's response:

> "Man: I choose you, my heart's delight,
> May our love grow ever bright.
> Lady: I choose you, my strength, my guide,
> With blessings from the Gods by our side."

The man places a ribbon on the Pentacle and says:

> "Bless this ribbon with love so deep,
> In our hearts, its bond we keep.
> With God's strength and Goddess's grace,
> May it hold our love in place."

He ties the ribbon around the lady's wrist. They kiss.

The lady then places the other ribbon on the Pentacle and says:

> "Bless this ribbon with love's pure light,
> Keeping our hearts ever bright.
> With Goddess's love and God's embrace,
> May it keep our bond in place."

She ties the ribbon around her partner's wrist. They kiss.

They turn to face the altar again. The man leads, followed by the lady:

> "Man: Goddess of love, so kind and fair,
> Thank you for your presence here.
> Lady: God of strength, so true and wise,
> We thank you for your guiding light."

Finish off the ceremony by closing the Circle.

Tarot Love Spell

REQUIREMENTS:

❀ Star card
❀ Lovers card
❀ King of Cups card
❀ Pink candle
❀ Cinnamon
❀ Pink quartz
❀ Red rose petals

INSTRUCTIONS:

Lay down the Star card. Close your eyes and visualize any obstacles that may keep you and your soulmate apart.

Place the King of Cups card next. Visualize everything you desire in your soulmate.

Finally, place the Lovers card in the center, positioning the pink candle on top.

Surround the candle with pink quartz and red rose petals, creating a sacred circle.

Light the pink candle, saying:

> "Flame of love, bright and true,
> Guide my heart in all I do."

Sprinkle cinnamon onto the flame and speak from your heart:

"Goddess of love, hear my plea,
Bring my soulmate close to me.
A love that's pure, a love that's true,
Let our hearts entwine anew.
This is my wish, this is my plea,
Bring us together, so mote it be."

Let the candle burn fully. Throughout the process, periodically return to sprinkle cinnamon on the flame, visualizing your heart opening and your soulmate drawing nearer. Let the scent of roses fill the air, symbolizing pure love and motherly guidance.

Once the candle has burned out, focus on your intent and visualize your soulmate clearly. Conclude by saying:

"With this spell, I seek your aid,
Show me the path love has made.
Goddess of love, hear my plea,
Guide my heart, so mote it be."

Venus's Love Embrace

REQUIREMENTS:

❧ One Red Heart Cloth
❧ One Red Candle
❧ One Mirror
❧ One White Cloth
❧ Seven Pins
❧ One Scent of Venus Incense Stick (or rose, basil, or lavender)
❧ Ylang Ylang oil for anointing

INSTRUCTIONS:

On a Friday evening, the sacred day of Venus, begin this enchanting spell. Repeat the ritual for seven nights in succession.

Begin with a cleansing ritual and a relaxing bath.

Anoint your body with Ylang Ylang oil, inviting the essence of love and attraction.

Select a magical area within your bedroom.

Lay out the white cloth and position yourself before the mirror.

Cast a protective circle around your sacred space.

Light the red candle and incense, allowing the fragrant smoke to fill the room.

Focus on your sexual energy and channel it into the spell.

Hold the red heart cloth in your hands and gaze into the mirror.

Chant with passion and intent:

"I call thee, beloved one,
To love me more than anyone.
Seven times I pierce thy heart,
Tonight the magic of Venus starts.
I bind thy heart and soul to me;
As I will it, so shall it be."

After each recitation of the chant, place one pin into the heart cloth.

Repeat this process until all seven pins are placed, chanting:

"Seven times I pierce thy heart."

Snuff out the candle and incense with reverence.

Leave the pins in the heart cloth until the next night's ritual.

Repeat this ritual for seven consecutive nights, each night piercing the heart anew, deepening the bond and invoking the power of Venus.

Waning Moon Love Ritual

REQUIREMENTS:

❀ Three glasses or chalices
❀ A small picture of two happy people (It doesn't need to be special; something from a magazine representing your goal works best.)
❀ A love-associated oil (such as rose, apple blossom, or vanilla; vanilla extract can be used)
❀ A candle in pink, red, or silver

INSTRUCTIONS:

Fill two of the chalices halfway with water and set them on opposite ends of your altar to symbolize two separate halves.

Place the empty chalice in the center of the altar.

Arrange the oil, picture, and other items conveniently.

Perfume the air with your chosen oil by anointing a working candle.

Visualize your goal as you prepare, projecting it into the candle.

Light the candle once you have cast your circle, letting it illuminate your work.

Chant:

> "Candle red (or silver or pink) as love light bright,
> Carry my prayers to the God & Goddess tonight."

Slow your mind and focus inward, visualizing the end of loneliness.

Form a mental picture of yourself alone, building a strong emotion of intolerance for this state.

Pour your deeply felt emotion into the mental image and, with a burst of will, send it far away into the universe, where it will harmlessly dissolve.

Focus on the empty center chalice, seeing it as potential waiting to be filled.

Invest the empty cup with your hopes and dreams of romance, companionship, love, and loyalty.

If you are female, the chalice on the left represents you; if male, the right chalice is yours.

Lift the chalice that represents you and the other, holding them as far apart as possible.

Feel your need pouring into yours, and the unknown person's need filling the other.

Look into the empty chalice, feeling loneliness melting away as it fills with loving potential.

Bring the two cups to your breast, sensing the energy within them striving to unite.

When the time feels right, pour the contents of the two chalices into the center one, feeling happiness and relief as the halves become whole.

Seal the union with a single drop of the chosen oil, allowing it to mingle with the joined waters.

Chant:

> "Separated at birth, full circle come,
> Two halves of wholeness are joined as one.
> With harm to none, leaving all choice free,
> By my will, so let it be."

Hold the picture over the chalice, transferring the joyful energy into the image.

Project your likeness and that of the one drawn to you onto the picture.

Place a drop of the water and another of the oil on the picture, fold it tightly, and carry it with you until the moon phase changes.

Burn the picture when the moon phase changes. If needed, repeat the spell on the next full moon.

Win the Heart of a Resistant Lover

REQUIREMENTS:

❖ Wax doll fashioned in the image of your desired person
❖ A fireproof container
❖ A small fire or heat source

INSTRUCTIONS:

Find a quiet, undisturbed area to perform your spell.

Set up your space with the wax doll and your fireproof container.

Shape the wax into a doll that resembles your desired person.

Inscribe their name upon the doll with a pin or sharp tool, infusing it with your intention.

Light a small fire or use a heat source within the fireproof container.

Hold the wax doll in your hands, visualizing the person you desire.

Feel your heart's longing and project it into the doll.

Begin melting the wax doll over the fire, and as it softens and liquefies, recite the following spell:

> "Wax and flame, by magic's art,
> Melt away the cold, hard heart.
> As you soften, love takes flight,
> Bring (Name)'s love to me this night."

Continue to focus on the doll melting, envisioning the person's heart softening and opening to you.

Let the wax fully melt away, representing the complete transformation of their feelings.

When the wax has melted entirely, whisper:

"By fire's glow and melted wax,
Love now flows, no turning back.
From rejection, love does grow,
As I will it, let it flow."

Safely extinguish the fire and allow the wax to cool.

Bury the remnants of the wax in the earth, symbolizing the grounding and solidifying of their newfound love for you.

Concoctions

Love and Admiration Oil

REQUIREMENTS:

❀ 20 drops musk
❀ 2 drops jasmine oil
❀ 1 drop ylang ylang oil
❀ 1 rose petal
❀ 1 small piece of crystal quartz
❀ 1/8 teaspoon powdered cinnamon
❀ A small glass bottle

INSTRUCTIONS:

Combine the musk, jasmine oil, and ylang ylang oil in the glass bottle.

Place this bottle where it will be bathed in the light of the full moon for three consecutive nights. Ensure you bring it inside before the sun rises each day to keep the lunar energy pure.

Set the rose petal, crystal quartz, and powdered cinnamon in a place where the sun's rays can touch them. Leave them in the sunlight during the day, and remove them before the moonlight can find them.

On the fourth day, combine the solar-infused rose petal, quartz, and cinnamon with the lunar-infused oils in the glass bottle. Seal the bottle tightly.

Create a sacred space where you will not be disturbed. Light a pink or red candle to represent love and attraction.

Hold the bottle in your hands, close your eyes, and visualize yourself radiating love and admiration. Feel the warmth of the sun and the mystery of the moon filling the oil with their power.

With intention and focus, recite the following incantation:

"*Moonlit nights and sunlit days,*
Bless this oil in wondrous ways.
Love and admiration flow,
From me, let their hearts bestow.
With musk and jasmine, ylang ylang's grace,
Draw affection to my space.
Rose, quartz, and cinnamon blend,
Admiration, love, and respect extend."

Apply a small amount of the enchanted oil to your pulse points whenever you wish to attract love and admiration.

Visualize yourself surrounded by a glowing aura of love and respect, knowing the oil is amplifying your natural charm and magnetism.

Store the oil in a dark, cool place when not in use. Remember to apply it with intention and gratitude, allowing the energies of the moon and sun to bring forth love and admiration into your life.

Love and Lust Oil

Use the oil to anoint yourself or a love charm when you wish to attract or enhance love and passion.

REQUIREMENTS:

❁ A small red bottle
❁ 12 or more red rose petals (heavily scented)
❁ Fresh sprig of peppermint
❁ Three cinnamon basil leaves
❁ Fresh sprig of parsley
❁ 1/2 tsp. each of the following herbs: caraway seeds, cloves, rosemary, yarrow, catnip
❁ Olive oil
❁ Essential oils: 6 drops each of rose geranium, lemon, orange, jasmine; 3 drops of vanilla oil
❁ Lavender flowers
❁ Red and pink candles
❁ Mortar and pestle

INSTRUCTIONS:

On the night of the new moon, gather your ingredients and tools.

Create a sacred space where you won't be disturbed.

Place the rose petals, peppermint, basil leaves, and parsley into the red bottle.

Using a mortar and pestle, grind the caraway seeds, cloves, rosemary, yarrow, and catnip to a coarse texture.

Add the ground herbs to the red bottle.

Pour olive oil into the herb mixture until the bottle is about 3/4 full.

In a separate small bottle, blend **6** drops each of rose geranium, lemon, orange, and jasmine oils, along with **3** drops of vanilla oil.

Add this blend of essential oils to the red bottle.

Add lavender flowers until the bottle is nearly full.

Shake the bottle gently to mix all the ingredients.

Light a red candle for passion and a pink candle for love.

Hold the bottle between your hands, close your eyes, and visualize the oil being infused with the energies of love and desire.

Chant the following incantation:

> "By the moon's new light, I blend this potion,
> With herbs and oils, a love-filled ocean.
> Rose and jasmine, lemon and spice,
> Bring forth passion, love's true delight.
> Lavender blooms, and mint so sweet,
> With every drop, our hearts shall meet.
> Cinnamon's warmth and vanilla's kiss,
> Seal this spell with a loving bliss.
> By candle's flame and moon's soft glow,
> Love and lust, through this oil, flow."

Let the candles burn down completely.

Store the oil in a dark, cool place.

Love and Lust Oil 2

REQUIREMENTS:

❀ A small red bottle
❀ 12 red rose petals
❀ A small sprig of peppermint
❀ 3 cinnamon-basil leaves
❀ A small sprig of parsley
❀ 1/2 tsp. caraway seed
❀ 1/2 tsp. cloves
❀ 1/2 tsp. rosemary
❀ 1/2 tsp. yarrow
❀ 1/2 tsp. catnip
❀ Olive oil
❀ 6 drops vanilla oil
❀ 6 drops rose oil
❀ 6 drops lemon oil
❀ 6 drops jasmine oil
❀ 6 drops orange oil
❀ Dried lavender buds

INSTRUCTIONS:

In a mortar, grind together the caraway seed, cloves, rosemary, yarrow, and catnip until finely blended.

Place the rose petals, peppermint sprig, cinnamon-basil leaves, and parsley sprig into the red bottle.

Add the ground herb mixture to the bottle, then fill it 3/4 full with olive oil.

Next, add the following essential oils while chanting:

"Vanilla, rose, lemon, jasmine, and orange,
Blend together with love's sweet chorus.
Stirring passion, stirring desire,
Ignite the flames of love's bright fire."

Add dried lavender buds to the bottle until it is full.

Cork the bottle tightly and let it steep, absorbing the energies and intentions you've infused.

Keep the bottle in a sacred space, using the oil to anoint yourself or objects to attract love and passion into your life.

Love Oil

REQUIREMENTS:

❈ 4 tablespoons Sweet Almond Oil or Safflower Oil
❈ 1/2 teaspoon Evening Primrose essential oil (optional)
❈ 1/2 teaspoon Carrot Seed essential oil (optional)
❈ 12 drops Sandalwood essential oil
❈ 6 drops Ylang Ylang essential oil
❈ 4 drops Clary Sage essential oil
❈ 2 drops Rose essential oil (for dark hair and skin)
❈ 2 drops Neroli essential oil (for light hair and skin)

INSTRUCTIONS:

In a shallow dish, pour **4** tablespoons of Sweet Almond Oil or Safflower Oil as the base.

Add **1/2** teaspoon of Evening Primrose essential oil and **1/2** teaspoon of Carrot Seed essential oil if desired.

Add **12** drops of Sandalwood essential oil, **6** drops of Ylang Ylang essential oil, and **4** drops of Clary Sage essential oil.

For dark hair and skin, add **2** drops of Rose essential oil. For light hair and skin, add **2** drops of Neroli essential oil.

Gently warm the base oil if it is not already at room temperature.

Slowly mix all the essential oils into the base oil, stirring clockwise, and focus your intent on drawing love and affection into your life.

Find a quiet, undisturbed area to perform your spell. Light some incense or a pink candle to create a loving atmosphere.

Take a moment to center yourself and ground your energy. Hold your hands over the dish of mixed oils and infuse them with your intention for love and attraction.

As you stir the oil clockwise, chant the following words three times:

"Oil of enchantment, blend and unite,
Draw to me love, both day and night.
Sandalwood, Ylang Ylang, Clary Sage,
Ignite the passion, set the stage."

Apply the oil to your body in small amounts, using comfortable pressure and working towards your heart. As you do so, visualize love surrounding you and coming into your life. Avoid the face and genital area.

Once you have finished applying the oil, thank the energies and entities you called upon. Close your sacred space and extinguish the candle or incense if used.

Chant:

"With this oil, love shall flow,
Into my life, let affection grow.
By this magic, strong and pure,
My heart's desires shall endure."

Keep the vial of love oil in a special place and use it whenever you wish to enhance your aura of attraction and love.

Love Oil 2

REQUIREMENTS:

❀ Orris root
❀ An earthen bowl
❀ Pure olive oil (half a cup)
❀ Jasmine oil (for women) or patchouli oil (for men)
❀ A pink cloth
❀ Pink candles

INSTRUCTIONS:

On a Friday evening when the Moon is waxing, lay a pink cloth on your altar.

Light the pink candles to illuminate your space with the glow of love.

Pour the orris root into the earthen bowl, then add half a cup of olive oil.

Stir with the forefinger of your dominant hand seven times clockwise.

Add three to seven drops of jasmine oil (for women) or patchouli oil (for men).

Place the bowl on the altar and gaze into it, visualizing your deepest desire for love.

Enchant the oil by chanting:

"Love, love, love, love, love, love, love."

Alternatively, recite a favorite love poem or sonnet to infuse the oil with your personal touch.

Pour the enchanted oil into a jar and cork it tightly.

Wrap the jar in the pink altar cloth and place it in a dark place for seven days.

On the following Friday night, uncork the bottle, strain the oil, and store it in the same bottle.

This Love Oil is to be worn only by its creator, keeping its magic pure and true.

Chant to Seal the Spell:

> "Oil of love, now enchant,
> Bring to me the love I chant.
> By moon's light and candle's glow,
> Love's sweet magic, let it flow."

Love Oil 3

Wear the magick love oil as a perfume to draw love to you. Anoint yourself with it before going out, or whenever you wish to enhance your aura of attraction.

REQUIREMENTS:

❁ 7 drops Palmarosa essential oil
❁ 5 drops Ylang Ylang essential oil
❁ 1 drop Ginger essential oil
❁ 2 drops Rosemary essential oil
❁ 1 drop Cardamom essential oil
❁ Pink candles

INSTRUCTIONS:

In a small glass vial, combine the essential oils: 7 drops of Palmarosa, 5 drops of Ylang Ylang, 1 drop of Ginger, 2 drops of Rosemary, and 1 drop of Cardamom. Swirl the vial gently to mix the oils together.

Take a pink candle and anoint it with the blended oil. As you do so, visualize the love you wish to attract into your life. See the energy of the oils infusing the candle with your intention.

Find a quiet, undisturbed place where you can perform the spell. Light some incense or play soft, soothing music if it helps you to focus.

Cast a protective circle around your space to create a sacred area for your spellwork.

Place the anointed pink candle in the center of your altar or a safe surface. Light the candle and let the flame represent the love you wish to draw into your life.

As the candle burns, focus on the flame and visualize love coming to you. Chant the following words three times:

> "Oils of love, blend and unite,
> Draw to me a love pure and bright.
> Flame of passion, warm and true,
> Bring a love that's meant to be, to me, to you."

Spend a few moments in quiet meditation, focusing on the warmth of the candle's flame and the scent of the oils filling the air. Envision the love you desire entering your life.

Once you feel the spell is complete, thank the energies and entities you called upon. Snuff out the candle (do not blow it out) and close the circle.

Chant:

> "With this oil, love I invite,
> Pure and gentle, shining bright.
> Love shall come, to fill my days,
> Guided by this candle's blaze."

Keep the vial of love oil in a special place and use it whenever you feel the need to attract love and affection into your life.

Love Potion

REQUIREMENTS:

❀ A few large apples
❀ Cinnamon
❀ Yarrow
❀ Spring water
❀ Salt
❀ An enameled or cast-iron saucepan

INSTRUCTIONS:

Gather the apples, cinnamon, yarrow, spring water, and salt.

Bless or consecrate these components if it aligns with your practice.

Focus your intention on attracting love and passion as you prepare the potion.

Slice the apples and place them into the saucepan.

Coat the apples with cinnamon, then cover with yarrow.

Add enough spring water to submerge the contents and sprinkle a pinch of salt.

Stir clockwise on low heat, chanting:

"Apple and spice, yarrow and sea,
Brew this potion, love come to me."

Bring the mixture to a gentle simmer for about 90 minutes.

Strain the potion and place the liquid into a dark jar.

Add a few drops of the potion to your favorite aftershave or cologne.

Wear it every four days to invoke the magic.

Remember, the magic endures even after the scent fades.

Chant to Seal the Spell:

"With this brew, love's flame ignite,
Attracting passion, pure delight.
By the magic in this potion made,
Love's allure shall never fade."

Love Tea for Two

REQUIREMENTS:

❈ 2 tsp. rose petals
❈ 1 tsp. spearmint herb
❈ 1 tsp. ground licorice root
❈ 1 tsp. hawthorn herb
❈ A pinch of coriander
❈ A pinch of cinnamon
❈ A pinch of nutmeg
❈ Vanilla or ginger honey to taste

INSTRUCTIONS:

Gather your ingredients and ensure your space is calm and serene.

Bring 3 cups of pure spring water to a rolling boil.

As the water boils, empower each herb and spice with your magical intent. Hold them in your hands and visualize love and warmth infusing into them.

Place the rose petals, spearmint, licorice root, hawthorn, coriander, cinnamon, and nutmeg into the boiling water.

Lower the heat and let the mixture simmer gently for 3 minutes, stirring clockwise as you infuse it with your intention of love and connection.

Remove the pot from heat and let the tea steep for an additional 5 minutes.

As the tea steeps, close your eyes and envision the loving energy of the herbs blending and growing stronger.

Strain the tea into two beautiful cups.

Add vanilla or ginger honey to taste, stirring each cup with a whispered chant:

> "Roses of love, mint of delight,
> Licorice sweet and hawthorn bright,
> Coriander, cinnamon, nutmeg's fire,
> Blend in harmony, fulfill desire.
> Honey's touch, love's pure art,
> Unite us now, heart to heart."

Sit with your beloved, and as you both drink the tea, feel the magic working within, bringing your hearts closer and deepening your bond.

Lover's Bath

REQUIREMENTS:

❀ 4 drops Ylang Ylang essential oil
❀ 2 drops Clary Sage essential oil
❀ 1 drop Bergamot essential oil
❀ 1 drop Sandalwood essential oil
❀ Candles
❀ Soft, romantic music

INSTRUCTIONS:

Gather all your ingredients and set them near the bathtub.

Light the candles around the bathroom to create a soft, romantic glow.

Play some soft, enchanting music to set the mood.

Fill the bathtub with warm water, ensuring it's at a comfortable temperature.

As the water fills, add the essential oils.

Swish the water gently with your hand, mixing the oils thoroughly.

Stand before the bath, close your eyes, and take a deep breath.

With intent and focus, recite the following spell:

"Waters of love, flow pure and bright,
Infuse this bath with passion tonight.
Ylang Ylang sweet, Clary Sage clear,
Bergamot's joy, Sandalwood near.
Candlelight gleams, music's soft tune,
Bring forth love's magic, beneath the moon.
As I bathe in this enchanted sea,
Love's true power, come to me."

Step into the bath, feeling the warmth and fragrance envelop you.

Soak in the magical waters, allowing the essential oils to infuse your skin and spirit.

Visualize love and passion flowing into your life, surrounding you with a warm glow.

Stay in the bath for as long as you feel comfortable, soaking in the love and light.

Once you feel ready, gently rise from the bath, letting the water drip away any negativity.

Thank the elements and energies for their presence and assistance.

Snuff out the candles, never blowing them out, to seal the spell.

Lust and Seduction Oil

Use this oil to anoint yourself, your lover, or objects to enhance attraction and seduction, invoking the energies of lust and desire with every drop.

REQUIREMENTS:

❀ 5 parts musk oil
❀ 5 parts civet oil
❀ 1 part ambergris oil
❀ 1 part patchouli or cassia oil

INSTRUCTIONS:

Gather all your ingredients in a quiet, sacred space where you can focus your intent.

In a small glass bottle, blend the oils in the proportions listed above.

As you mix each oil, chant the following incantation to infuse the blend with your desires:

> "Musk and civet, dark and deep,
> Ignite the fire that lies asleep.
> Ambergris, with essence rare,
> Enchant and lure with fragrant air.
> Patchouli (or cassia), warm and sweet,
> Seduction's spell shall now complete.
> Blend these oils, magic divine,
> Lust and passion now entwine."

Once all the oils are blended, hold the bottle in your hands and envision your desired outcome: intense passion and seduction.

Seal the bottle and store it in a special place.

NOTES

Passion Elixir

REQUIREMENTS:

✻ 1 pinch rosemary
✻ 2 pinches thyme
✻ 2 tsp. black tea
✻ 1 pinch coriander
✻ 3 fresh mint leaves (or 1/2 tsp. dried)
✻ 5 fresh rosebud petals (or 1 tsp. dried)
✻ 5 fresh lemon tree leaves (or 1 tsp. dried lemon peel)
✻ 3 pinches nutmeg
✻ 3 pieces orange peel
✻ Honey (optional, for sweetness)

INSTRUCTIONS:

Prepare your space with calm energy, perhaps lighting a candle or burning some incense to set the mood.

As you place each herb into the teapot, infuse them with your magical intention. Visualize the passion and love that you wish to bring into your life or relationship.

Boil 3 cups of pure spring water.

Pour the boiling water into the teapot over the herbs, envisioning a vibrant energy being released from each ingredient, combining to form a powerful elixir.

Let the mixture steep for a few moments, allowing the magical properties to meld and strengthen.

As the elixir steeps, close your eyes and chant softly:

"Herbs of passion, herbs of might,
Blend together on this night.
Love and desire, pure and true,
Ignite the flames, old and new."

Strain the elixir into beautiful cups.

If desired, sweeten with honey, stirring clockwise while focusing on the warmth and passion you wish to invoke.

Share the enchanted passion elixir with your beloved or enjoy it yourself, feeling the magical energies working within, stirring feelings of love and desire.

Sip this magical aphrodisiac passion drink slowly, allowing its enchanted flavors to awaken your senses and strengthen the bonds of love and passion within your heart.

Romance Magnet Oil

REQUIREMENTS:

❈ 2 drops ylang ylang oil
❈ 2 drops sandalwood oil
❈ 2 drops clary sage oil
❈ A pink candle

INSTRUCTIONS:

Combine the ylang ylang oil, sandalwood oil, and clary sage oil to create your Romance Magnet Oil.

Rub the Romance Magnet Oil onto the pink candle, infusing it with your desire for love and harmony.

Light the pink candle and chant:

"With oils of love and flame so bright,
Draw to me romance's light.
For three hours each day, I burn this fire,
Bringing closer my heart's desire."

Burn the candle for three hours each day.

If you seek new love, continue this ritual until a potential lover appears.

If you wish to enhance an existing relationship, end the ritual when harmony is restored.

Always snuff the candle rather than blowing it out to keep the spirit in the flame alive and your wish intact.

Chant as you snuff the flame:

> "Spirit of flame, remain with me,
> Guard my wish, let it be."

Trust in the magic of the oils and the flame to draw love into your life or to bring harmony to your relationship.

Chant to Seal the Spell:

> "By flame and oil, love's light be,
> Drawn to me, so mote it be."

Rose Geranium and Lavender Love Anointing Oil

REQUIREMENTS:

❀ One-eighth cup of unscented oil
❀ Rose geranium essential oil
❀ Lavender essential oil
❀ Clear glass jar
❀ Pink candle

INSTRUCTIONS:

In a clear glass jar, mix one-eighth cup of unscented oil with enough rose geranium and lavender oils to create a pleasant scent.

Empower the oil by focusing on the jar and thinking of the feelings of love—contentment, commitment, joy. Allow this love energy to flow into the oil.

Rub the oil well into the pink candle, infusing it with your intention to find love.

Find a quiet moment when you can be undisturbed for the duration of the candle's burn. Set up your space with the pink candle and your empowered oil.

Hold the pink candle in your hands, close your eyes, and visualize the love you wish to attract. Feel the emotions of happiness, contentment, and joy.

Light the candle and say the following prayer with sincerity and focus:

"Oh Lady of love, and Lord so strong,
Guide my heart where it belongs.
Bring to me my destined one,
By moon and stars, let love be spun.
With no harm done, no will coerced,
I seek my true love, for better or worse.
Grateful am I, with heart so pure,
Let love find me, let it endure."

Allow the candle to burn fully. As it does, visualize your true love drawing closer to you with each passing moment.

When the candle has burned out completely, your spell is complete. Trust that the energies you have set forth will bring your true love to you in due time.

Spellbound Love Potion

REQUIREMENTS:

❀ Filtered water
❀ 2 cups of red wine
❀ 1 teaspoon each of the following herbs: Cumin, Mint, and Peppermint

INSTRUCTIONS:

Light a red candle and some incense to set the mood for your love spell. Arrange your ingredients on the altar with intention.

Hold your hands over the herbs and wine, visualizing love and passion filling each ingredient. Chant:

> "Herbs of love and passion's fire,
> Ignite the heart, fulfill desire.
> Wine so red, with magic bound,
> Let love's enchantment now be found."

Combine the cumin, mint, and peppermint in a pot. Pour in the filtered water.

Set the pot over a flame, bringing the mixture to a boil. As it heats, stir clockwise, saying:

> "By water's boil and herbal blend,
> Let love's true magic now ascend.
> With each stir, let passion grow,
> As above, so below."

After ten minutes of simmering, pour in the red wine. Stir gently, visualizing your desired love coming to fruition.

As the potion simmers, recite:

> "Wine and herbs, in cauldron blend,
> A lover's heart to me now send.
> By this potion, hearts align,
> Love's true essence, intertwined."

Pour the potion into beautiful goblets. As you serve, whisper:

> "With every sip, let love unfold,
> Warm and tender, strong and bold.
> Drink and feel love's magic flow,
> As within, so love shall grow."

Extinguish the candle and give thanks to the spirits of love for their assistance. Drink the potion with your beloved, letting the magic of the herbs and wine bind your hearts together.

Winter Passion Drink

REQUIREMENTS:

❀ 6 fresh mint leaves
❀ 1/2 cup of rose petals
❀ 1 tablespoon each of clove and nutmeg
❀ 1/3 cup of bay leaves
❀ A pinch of coriander
❀ 1/2 cup of lemon and orange peel
❀ 4 cups of filtered water
❀ 1 bottle of red wine

INSTRUCTIONS:

Light a red candle and some incense to create a magical ambiance. Arrange your ingredients on the altar with intention.

Hold your hands over the herbs, water, and wine, visualizing warmth and passion filling each ingredient. Chant:

"Herbs and spices, pure and fine,
Blend with water, fruit, and wine.
Passion's flame within this brew,
Ignite love's fire, strong and true."

Combine the mint leaves, rose petals, clove, nutmeg, bay leaves, coriander, and lemon and orange peel in a large pot.

Pour in the filtered water and bring the mixture to a boil. Stir clockwise, chanting:

> "Water's essence, pure and clear,
> Blend with spices, bring love near.
> As you boil, let passions rise,
> Underneath the winter skies."

Reduce the heat and let the mixture simmer for **15** minutes. As it simmers, chant:

> "By clove and mint, by rose and bay,
> Bring forth love, night and day.
> Coriander, citrus, blend so bright,
> Ignite the heart, with passion's light."

Pour in the red wine, stirring gently. Visualize the love and warmth filling the potion, chanting:

> "Wine so red, with magic bound,
> Let love's enchantment now be found.
> In every sip, let passion flow,
> As above, so below."

Pour the magic drink into beautiful goblets. As you serve, whisper:

> "With each sip, let warmth unfold,
> Love and passion, strong and bold.
> Drink and feel love's magic blend,
> Hearts entwined, till winter's end."

Extinguish the candle and give thanks to the spirits of love and passion for their assistance. Drink the potion with your beloved, letting the magic of the herbs and wine bind your hearts together and keep the winter chill at bay.

Books by this Author

- The Protection Bible - The Essential Book of Protection Spells and Magic
- The Essential Book of Binding Spells and Magic
- The Essential Book of Cleansing, Blessing, and Purification Spells and Magic
- The Essential Book of Healing Spells and Magic
- The Essential Book of Household Spells and Magic
- The Essential Book of Love Spells and Magic

More Books by Erebus Society

The Standard Book of Candle Magic

by K.P. Theodore

In The Standard Book of Candle Magic you will learn about the use of candles in magical traditions, the meanings of colours so you can create your own candle magic rituals, how to prepare for magical practice, how to cast a standard circle, and over 30 Candle Magic spells for your everyday magical needs.

The Standard Book of Meditation

by K.P. Theodore

Within the pages of this book, you will find a diverse array of meditation techniques waiting to be explored. From breath awareness to body scan, loving-kindness to visualization, the author has meticulously assembled a rich tapestry of practices that invite you to embark on a transformative inner journey.

Wandlore -
A Guide for the Apprentice Wandmaker
by K.P. Theodore

Delve into the ancient and intricate art of wandmaking with this comprehensive guide to the origins, properties, and crafting of magick wands. This book serves as both an introduction to wandlore and a hands-on manual for those who aspire to become skilled wand makers.

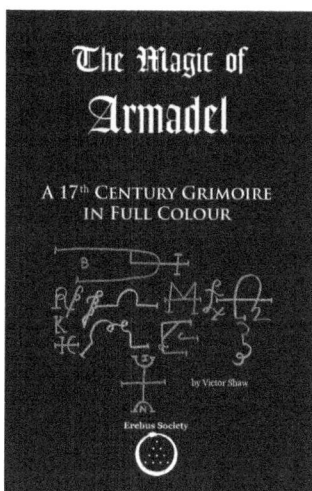

The Magic of Armadel - A 17th Century Grimoire in Full Colour
by Victor Shaw

The Grimoire of Armadel is a book of Celestial Magick and contains information, seals, and sigils of Angels, Demons and other Celestial Spirits.

It is classed as a Christian/Theistic Grimoire, and it was first translated by S.L. McGregor Mathers in the late 1890's from the original French and Latin manuscript that can be found in the Biblotheque l'Arsenal in Paris.

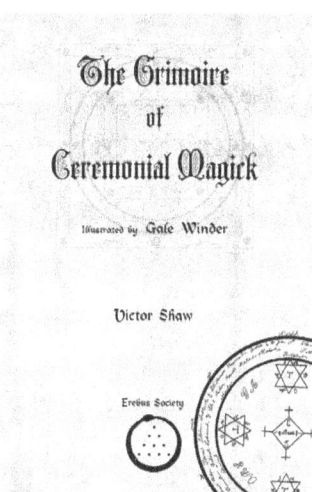

The Grimoire of Ceremonial Magick
by Victor Shaw

This book is a collection of passages, rites, practices, and rituals from various famous Grimoires. It is a cluster of the most obscure and powerful invocations, ceremonies, and pacts, and it explains their history and origins while it refutes certain myths surrounding Ancient Grimoires, and discusses the theology therein.

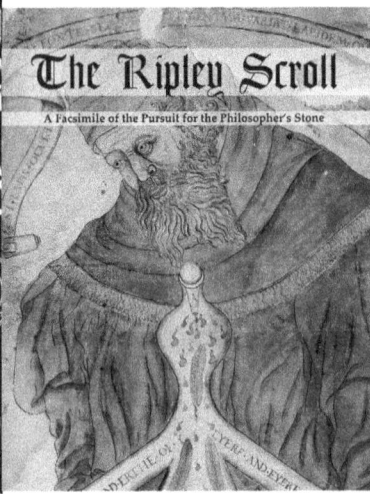

The Ripley Scroll: A Facsimile of the Pursuit for the Philosopher's Stone

by Victor Shaw

The 'Ripley scroll' or 'Ripley Scrowle' is a paramount alchemical work of the 15th century as it depicts the mystical and laborious process for the pursuit of the Philosopher's Stone. A legendary substance that can turn base metals into gold and can also be used in the making of the elixir of life, providing its possessor with prolonged life or even Immortality.

The Fundamental Book of Sigil Magick

by K.P. Theodore

This book serves as a textbook for those who wish to study the art of Sigil Magick. In its pages you will find information about the different kinds of sigils, their use, activation techniques and how to create custom tailored sigils from scratch.

Learn how to captivate emotions, empower the mind, create mental barriers, re-program the brain and alter consciousness by the use of "Mental Sigils".

The Accelerated Necromancer

by Gavin Fox

Necromancy has long been misunderstood, reduced to taboo and superstition. In this insightful work, Gavin redefines the practice, blending witchcraft and chaos magick to offer a responsible, spiritually enriching path.

With practical techniques, seasonal rites, and a fresh take on working with the dead, this book is a must-read for those seeking to walk the shadows with wisdom and reverence.

www.ingramcontent.com/pod-product-compliance
Lightning Source LLC
LaVergne TN
LVHW011207080426
835508LV00007B/654